The Seasons
WINTER

Written by Stephanie Hedlund • Illustrated by Stephanie Bauer

magic wagon

visit us at www.abdopublishing.com

Printed in the United States of America, North Mankato, Minnesota.
052013
012014
♻ This book contains at least 10% recycled materials.

Written by Stephanie Hedlund
Illustrated by Stephanie Bauer
Edited by Rochelle Baltzer
Cover and interior layout and design by Neil Klinepier

Library of Congress Cataloging-in-Publication Data

Hedlund, Stephanie F., 1977-
    Winter / by Stephanie Hedlund ; illustrated by Stephanie Bauer.
        pages cm -- (The seasons)
    ISBN 978-1-61641-995-0
    1. Winter--Juvenile literature. I. Bauer, Stephanie, illustrator. II. Title.
    QB637.8.H44 2014
    508.2--dc23
                        2012049769

Contents

Winter

There are four seasons during the year.
Do you know what season is first?
That's right, it is winter!
Then comes spring, summer, and autumn.

winter

spring

summer

Autumn

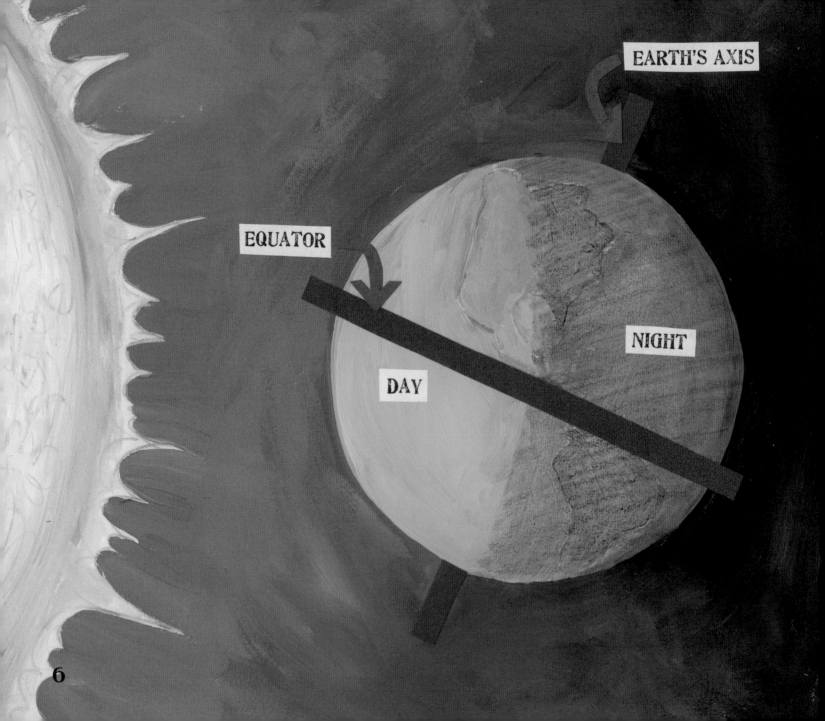

EARTH'S AXIS

EQUATOR

NIGHT

DAY

6

Why?

Earth travels around the sun during the year.
When Earth is tilted away from the sun, it is winter.
The days are shorter when the sun is farther away.
The shortest day is the **winter solstice**.
It falls on either December 21 or 22.

When?

Every year from December until March it is winter.
Unless you live below the **equator**!
Then winter comes from June until September.

Some areas have longer winters.
The **poles** are tilted away from the sun for months.
So, winter is longer near the poles.
Near the **equator**, winter only lasts for a month or two.

12

What's It Like Out?

Winter is the coldest season of them all.
The sky is often grey.
Some places get snow.
Some people even see ice and icicles!

Other places stay warm.
But they aren't as warm as in summer!

What Do They Do?

In winter, some plants are **dormant**.
Many trees are bare.
Only **evergreens** stay green and grow.

Some animals **hibernate**.
They find dens to rest in.
Others leave for the season.
They **migrate** in autumn.

People dress warm and go outdoors.
They go to school, sled, skate, ski, and have fun.
Soon, it will be spring!
Do you know what will happen then?

Seasons

January — Winter
February — Winter
March — Winter Spring
April — Spring
May — Spring
June — Spring Summer

Winter Activities

Build a Snowman

Go Ice Skating

Catch a Snowflake on your tongue

Write a Letter to Santa

Go Sledding

Make a Snow Angel

Build a Snow Fort

Web Sites

To learn more about the seasons, visit ABDO Group online. Web sites about the seasons are featured on our Book Links page. These links are routinely monitored and updated to provide the most current information available.

www.abdopublishing.com

Glossary

dormant - not active for a short time.

equator - an imaginary circle around the middle of Earth. It splits Earth into two equal parts.

evergreen - having leaves or needles that remain green through more than one season.

hibernate - to sleep or rest during the winter months.

migrate - to move from one place to another to find food or have babies.

pole - either end of the imaginary line that goes through an object. Each end of the line is an opposite.

winter solstice - (WIN-tehr SAHL-stehs) the shortest day of the year. The winter solstice usually occurs on December 21 or 22.

Index